OUR EARLIEST TATTOOS

**ETEL ADNAN
POETRY SERIES**

Edited by
Hayan Charara and Fady Joudah

Other Titles in This Series

the magic my body becomes | Jess Rizkallah

OUR EARLIEST TATTOOS

poems by **PETER TWAL**

The University of Arkansas Press
Fayetteville
2018

ISBN: 978–1–68226–072–2
e-ISBN: 978–1–61075–646–4

22 21 20 19 18   5 4 3 2 1

Designed by Liz Lester

♾ The paper used in this publication meets the minimum requirements of the American National Standard for Permanence of Paper for Printed Library Materials Z39.48-1984.

Library of Congress Control Cataloging-in-Publication Data

Names: Twal, Peter Samir Jeries, author.
Title: Our earliest tattoos : poems / by Peter Twal.
Description: Fayetteville : University of Arkansas Press, 2018. | Includes
    bibliographical references. |
Identifiers: LCCN 2018005248 (print) | LCCN 2018007826 (ebook) | ISBN
    9781610756464 (electronic) | ISBN 9781682260722 (pbk. : alk. paper)
Classification: LCC PS3620.W425 (ebook) | LCC PS3620.W425 A6 2018 (print) |
    DDC 811/.6--dc23
LC record available at https://urldefense.proofpoint.com/v2/url?u=https-3A__lccn
.loc.gov_2018005248&d=DwIFAg&c=7ypwAowFJ8v-mw8AB-SdSueVQg
SDL4HiiSaLK01W8HA&r=4fo1OqKuv_3krqlYYqNQWNKNaWxXN20G1
PCOL-2ERgE&m=UUZcxxuhoVIMwNvRowT3R4wD3H_lzOhW7u0toqe5ut
Q&s=NRwNtagWuLtTvNRRWuBd01kS4cexPMfr8WOrQWHxLbg&e=

for Jordy

SERIES EDITORS' PREFACE

The New Princeton Encyclopedia of Poetry and Poetics brings its entry on the sonnet to a close by noting its extraordinary stability despite the form's astonishing innovations over the past several hundred years. Fittingly, if not ironically, the entry ends with an expression of optimism, a quote from a poet, and a reference to death:

> This adaptability within a tradition of eight centuries' standing suggests that there will be no diminution of interest in and use of the form in the foreseeable future, and that the inherent difficulties that have kept the numbers of truly fine sonnets to an extremely small percentage of those written will deter neither versifier or genius from testing for her- or himself the challenge of what Rossetti called "a moment's monument,— / Memorial from the Soul's eternity / To one dead deathless hour."

Peter Twal appears to have succeeded not only in reinvigorating the form but also in adding his voice ("I sidearm you ears into the lake / like stones") to that "extremely small percentage" of poets to whose sonnet-conversation we should care to listen. In *Our Earliest Tattoos*, his debut poetry book, Twal's sonnet is his operating system. In the age of Twitter, of which pithiness and a quick wit (sometimes regarded as instantaneous wisdom) are hallmarks, this form is Twal's preferred media platform, his echo.

His truly is an "American" sonnet (as characterized by the Academy of American Poets), "identified by the ghost imprint that haunts it, recognizable by the presence of 14 lines or even by name only." Twal doesn't abandon form. Instead, he disguises the sonnet's formal properties, rendering them barely perceptible to the casual reader. To the more careful reader though, or the practitioner, these poems will evoke satisfaction, appreciation, perhaps even astonishment, but they will also doubtlessly call forth demurral. Poetry that takes risks always does.

As if anticipating such an argument, the opening poem, "It's the Memory of Our Betters," reminds us that "*The torch has been passed down,*" but "the sun sighs, smothered / beneath the rubble."

Whatever else lies beneath the rubble, the sonnet lives and breathes, as ghost or phoenix, reincarnated or refurbished for the twenty-first century. Whatever the architecture of the sonnet, Twal provides the reader with concrete tools and invented evidence to fill in the blanks. His poetic energy combines the absurd with the grave, the hilarious with the profound, the wacky with the tragic. In driving lines filled with unrelenting rhythms, his concerns engage the gray zone where the injured, mortal self is also fraudulent, decadent.

> I wonder if   a burning house, the wallpaper
> melting, is the most beautiful place to be colorblind

Through creative lexicon and constructed protagonists left noticeably incomplete, estranged, fabricated yet unquestionably real, the poet impersonates himself: the gifted American in his best suit at the gala of originality:

> These holes I burrow in the thick   sponge before stuffing
> my country   between my ribs, its wild
>
> wriggling, a fish
> caught in my eyelashes
> & this, the cigarette I offer to share
> That I'd even take the end on fire

In the book's opening poem, Twal places us in the museum of the Anthropocene: a blue jay whose imaginary extinction is a migration to the moon, and a sun subjugated to the history of a lightbulb exhibit. As Death makes its first appearance, it sets a tone:

always shoulder-to-shoulder with paradoxical grandiosity (a "supernova nostalgia," that "trades in [its] scythe for a cell phone"). And to this largesse, "the personified universe, that pile of phantom/ limbs" issues a request: *"Please no more/ dick pics."*

The phantom limbs announce a presence or, we dare say, a character, one of many that stand in for the numerous voices, ours, that speak through the poems—all of us elusive, nebulous, a clan of Hamm (as in Beckett's *Endgame*) trapped in a lyric whirlwind: the Mars Rover, a green turtle, tattoos, bleeding ghosts, toy soldiers, *do you copy*, and more. Their recurrences do not form a plot. They insist on a thrilling, morbidly comical ride through the wonderland of nonsense, whose vehicle is the clear-eyed swerving sentence.

> Looking for signs of life,
>
> the Mars Rover snaps
> a picture of us & Death   with this disquieting text:
>
> *Using your comb*
> *on my inner thigh right now*

As you hurtle along the pathways of Twal's art, one clearly feels that the two prominent voices here are Love and Death, "[n]one other than a sex thing   donning civil war faces":

> *I'm still a breath*   though I've lost my hand
>
> pressing into the wet cement of your heart   longer than I should

Regardless of the theme taken up (Ethos and Thanatos, language and trauma, politics and technology), after so many centuries—millennia, really—of poetic invention and reinvention, we return to the most basic desire of human nature, the most important product of aesthetic practice: feeling. *Our Earliest Tattoos* is replete with feelings, and because of this, you, too, will soften in the astonishing tenderness of these poems.

> If I have to   relearn   my body I will
> with a mother's amazement   clapping together her baby's feet
>
> If with a mother's amazement clapping together her baby's feet
> I relearn my body—

Hayan Charara and Fady Joudah

ACKNOWLEDGMENTS

Many thanks to the following anthology & magazines for publishing poems from this manuscript, sometimes in earlier versions, before anyone else:

The Believer, "Except in Parts"; *Berkeley Poetry Review*, "You Think Over & Over 'Hey, I'm Finally Dead'"; *Best New Poets*, "Made a Fool on the Road"; *Booth*, "Weather, Then You Picked the Wrong Place to Stay"; *Columbia Poetry Review*, "You Forgot What You Meant When You Read What You Said," "If I Could See All My Friends Tonight" (from page 55), "Sewed into Submission," & "Back to Your House"; *Connotation Press: An Online Artifact*, "The Conversation's Winding Away," "If You're Worried about the Weather," "You Drop the First Ten Years Just as Fast as You Can," "It's Better When We Pretend," "You Always Knew You were Tired"; *Crab Creek Review*, "If It's Crowded, All the Better" & "Oh, This Could be the Last Time So Here"; *cream city review*, "Leave Impossible Tasks"; *Devil's Lake*, "If I Could See All My Friends Tonight" (from page 54); *DIAGRAM*, "There's Always This"; *Forklift, Ohio*, "If the Sun Comes Up," & "I Wouldn't Trade One Stupid Decision"; *Gulf Coast*, "The Moral Kicks In"; *The Journal*, "It's the Memory of Our Betters" (as "Like a Sales Force into the Night"). *Kenyon Review Online*, "One of the Ways We Show Our Age"; *New Delta Review*, "Like a Sales Force into the Night" (as "It's the Memory of Our Betters"). *Ninth Letter*, "People Who Are Trying to Be Polite"; *Pleiades*, "I Still Don't Want to Stagger Home"; *Public Pool*, "Days in the Middle," "Where are Your Friends Tonight" (from page 50), & "Stand, You Can Sleep on the Plane"; *Quarterly West*, "Where are Your Friends Tonight" (from page 51); *RHINO*, "Made a Fool on the Road" (as "On the Road"). *Third Coast*, "Where are Your Friends Tonight" (from page 49); *Tinderbox Poetry Journal*, "Come Apart in Your Hand" & "Up Late but If You're Worried"; *West Branch Wired*, "We Set Controls for the Heart," & "Come Home to This & with a Face"; *Wildness*, "If I Could See All My

Friends Tonight" (from page 52) & "If I Could See All My Friends Tonight" (from page 53); *Yemassee*, "Years Trying to Get with the Plan & the Next Five Years."

With all that I am, thank you to:

God.

My parents, Samir & Helen—Baba, for carrying me down the stairs those many Saturday mornings & for carrying me now in more ways than you can know; Mama, for teaching me to be honest, respectful, & good—I will always look up to you, no matter our height disparity; My sister Sarah, for your unending friendship & for screaming my name when you were the only one to see me fall into that pool way, way back; Zeid, for being a gentleman & a generous soul, always laughing, refilling my glass, & making me laugh; Max, habibi, you've grown this family so much with such a little body.

For the life you give me, my stateside family & everyone in Jordan: Nana (Allah yerhamha), Khalto Nancy, Khalto Nahida, Amo Imad, Reem, Dana, Andy, Jakob, Nader, Michelle, Mekiah, Ameen, Jonathan, Khalto Aida, Amo Kamal (Allah yerhamo) for giving so much to this book, Tarek, Rula, Michelle, Nicole, Zeid, Mariam, Zed, Khalo Ramzy, Marlene, Khalo Khalid, Bayda, Emily, Kyle, Amameh Samirah, Amo Sami, Aunty Nabila, Jeries, Raghda, Samantha, Joyce, Suhad, Ghali, Rasheed, Ghazal, Wassem, Mod, Nassam, Zeinah, Amo Toufic, Aunty Yolla, Roy, Ralph, & all others. You helped raise me, fed me all kinds of heavenly food, always let me tag along, danced with me at weddings knowing I was a mess of a dancer, asked if I was still writing, & never told me it was time to put away my art.

For making room for me in your family with a love so moving I can't help but feel I was a part of it before I ever walked through your door, not laughing too much as I struggled to keep up at crawfish boils, accepting my eccentricities & teaching me yours. Most importantly though, for sharing Erin with me: Mrs. Barbara, Mr. Mike,

Jess, Bentley, Colin, Isabel, Ellie, Levi, Nicole, Blake, Uncle Chris, Uncle Jim (Allah yerhamo), & Mrs. Lil (Allah yerhamha).

Greyhouse & coffee.

For Friday nights at Cedar House, dance parties, flesh fiction readings, two of my best years & my whole Notre Dame experience, the love you invested in my many drafts & me: Leo, Ali, Beth, Alice, Jayme, Jenica, Lynda, Kaushik, Emily, Christine, Mari, Kuma, Coleen, Orlando, Johannes, Jim, Don, Chris, Anne, & Joyelle. Susan, for your incredible positivity & wisdom, your strength that becomes mine. Laura, Lara, Blake Lee, Taylor, Laura, Hatem, & Corey from LSU. & Brock for believing in me first, letting me into your class even though it was at capacity. I'm so glad you ruined my life with poetry.

Some of the most exemplary humans I'll ever know to whom I owe debts that cannot be repaid: Jordy, I miss you more deeply every day. Moreed, Hamid, James, Steven, Wil, Elizabeth, Blakeley, Bashar, Mohammad, Shoko, Elliott, Siwar, Samih, Dan, Priya, Mike, Kenny, Mrs. Anna, my Site Savers for life (Jill, Matt, & Nick), Drew, Fielding, Kyle, Adam, Jacob, Brittany, Patrick, Ricky, Ashley, Joe, Lindsey, Jake, Carrie, Ellery, Stacey, & Jeff. Round after round of Smash Bros., inning after inning of backyard baseball, song after song, terrible poem after terrible poem. Where would I be without your kindness, your inimitable love that teaches me to better love myself?

All the folks at Kongsberg Maritime & ECN whose friendship & intellects propel me forward, challenge me to grow as an engineer & a thinker. In particular, Feras, Adrian, Michael, Krzysztof, Johnathan, Rashaad, Andrew, Ethan, Gail, Ralph, Goodlett, Remender, Maden, Mason, Jerry G., Jerry R., Ben, Sundeep, Robin, Dave, Doug, Shawn, Michelle, LJ, Indy, Muffley, T.J., Sarah, Glen, & Al. It will remain one of my greatest honors, working beside each of you, & you can't know the joy it's been to break bread & other things in your company.

LCD Soundsystem, for calling it quits & getting back together. For some of my favorite music forever & closing your show with "All My Friends."

Though I am doomed to inadequately express it—Fady & Hayan. Your generosity, incredible insight, & selfless care for me & this book have brought my art to life in ways I never understood. It is a dream to call you friends. Immense gratitude to the Radius of Arab American Writers for carving out this space for writers of Arab heritage & defending it, & the University of Arkansas Press, DS, Melissa, Charlie, Molly, Anthony, Liz, Mike, for your time, talents, & support.

Etel Adnan for creating & creating.

You, Erin. You & you & you. Heart of my heart, greatest adventure. I will never know the words, and I hope I never do. Every ounce of love I could possibly muster is for you.

CONTENTS

ONE

It's the Memory of Our Betters

On the moon, a blue jay, unsure   where it last left its nest

prays to Saint Anthony while on earth   someone incorrectly

adjusts a thermostat   & a museum   of natural history explodes—   creating

more natural history   Lost in awe in a light bulb

exhibit, reading every last placard, the sun explodes   as well, a pimple

from a Hubble away & yet: *The torch has been passed down*, the sun sighs, smothered

beneath the rubble   Death comes to us full-

bellied but always craving   & the next time architects resurrect the museum,

precautions are taken to protect the art: *Patrons   please don't*

bleed on the paintings   & I force myself   to enjoy

this cappuccino in the frozen atrium   nothing like the natural

light my body stomachs, a funnel

stretched down my throat   in a vacuum   like the blue jay

back on the moon, eventually bluer than it was born to be

TWO

Like a Sales Force into the Night

In this montage sequence   you, more than ever, become
my supernova nostalgia   with all those disposable cameras

strapped to your chest   flashing in unison   Your cellophane
skin expands   expounds upon the mystery
of comedic timing   Somewhere in the city: Death

trades in his scythe for a cell phone   skinny pants painted on,
cloak left in the closet   *Please no more*
dick pics   says the personified universe, that pile of phantom
limbs   in the mirror, buffing out steam   Following a strobe

light shower   everything shines
like the afterlife   Watching you   skeet-shoot aerosol cans
from the roof of your garage   the night before

your very own meteor swarm   & my texts
the blurred things they were saying at the time

I Wouldn't Trade One Stupid Decision

For the next two days, my head like a red cup, a whole
constellation scattered across the floor   How I got this insignificant
card in my coat saying   *Hello*

I'm suffering from the worst case of TV snow shadow
this side of the cul-de-sac   is beyond me, but still I take

donations   Between the couch cushions,
my keys   crumpled up, your rusted hair
pin, a thousand more   steps forward pull me back like a train
halting & then my head   A bathroom stall
with my portrait painted on is where
I found this zipperless heart

forever binge-breathing   Was I swallowing

stars for warmth last night   or
licking your temporary tattoos

Made a Fool on the Road

& when I awake   *Dear Diary,*   *Tuscaloosa: Death*
came to me last night, a couple   *exits early*   *cut my hair crooked in my sleep*   *So that's*

fine   Snow beginning to stick   A radio personality dying into a million pieces
& because of the broken-paned solitude, I   read a book
about solitude   in a cave, atop a canyon, in echoes of a mother
drowning farther & farther away   Then I find a rest stop   I eat the book

feeling by feeling   the piecewise way we forget
people   cutting them up, hiding the memories in our freezers   I take note: *Today's*
is the exact number of times I can be yanked from myself   *by some long oily arm*
before I forget   *whether I am the arm or the toy soldier*   *the placeholder*

the excuse   In between strangled radio stations, a car
backfires next to me, or an atom miles away   splits
the life expectancy of a billboard   & a text
from you about finding my phantom limb   in the back seat of your car   *Thanks for that*

One of the Ways We Show Our Age

You vibrate the littlest bone in my ear   & drive
from the couch   flicking radio knobs to pick up
the frequency of your white
teeth, violins   grinding against

each other   The echo from my chesthole says   *Whatever happened*
to that surgery channel will happen to us all

Maybe we're just birds   trapped
in an airport   I can't stop scratching
the back of my ear   I can't stop crying   for help every time I flip
the channel but   you tell me parallel parking
hurts   & your hands circle

the air like a buzzsaw   spitting
slightly as you speak:
Holy water   holy water

Years Trying to Get with the Plan & the Next Five Years

Even the Mars Rover will run   out of the curiosity
required to show up to a game of charades, clenching a bag of actual blood
Just like you, my reanimated corpse, violence of memory, the Frankenstein
come to kill me & unraveling   into the invisibility of time

What I would give   *to oxidize your eyes to the gorgeous rust*
from whence they came   before transmission

is lost: the Mars Rover spending a half-life
thumbing through pictures on its phone   the earth forever
blinking & blushing & the performance of a lifetime: seeing you
step on an IED in my living
room   a crater for God

who always shows up late with something
green between   his teeth
& no one has the heart   to tell Him

People Who Are Trying to Be Polite

A dog in the dark
shadow of your self-portrait, you
snap off my arm   in black, sight
blurry,   waterboarding me & another & another & *here, I've saved you*

the last bite of this grenade   I'm not asking
you to survive this
breath of   closet fire   our bones tangled, braided
smoke clouds overhead   I am asking you to live with me   Even if that tattoo
won't fit on my face   Even if you don't notice
the fresh pair of lungs   I don every day

These holes I burrow in the thick   sponge before stuffing
my country   between my ribs, its wild

wriggling, a fish
caught in my eyelashes

& this, the cigarette I offer to share
That I'd even take the end on fire

Come Apart in Your Hand

A mountain of skin cells & a dented shadow   My past
self   develops overexposed in every shot   Left to steep

far too long, your body soddens, wades in the lake
of my oldest memory, but in this cagey head

which of us is   the bloodthirsty   The farther back   the eggier the screaming

in my ears   Could I be more obvious if I finger-paint you
stick-figured inside my cheeks   chased through town by some large   (but no less
dead) mammal?   I pick my teeth with the boniest   beliefs, but you don't

know the faces I make in the dark   The pop I play on repeat when no one's
coming home   *I'm still a breath*   though I've lost my hand
pressing into the wet cement of your heart   longer than I should

If the Sun Comes Up

If we played hide-&-go-seek
without bones
If always a piece of you
crammed in the cupboard
If all my friends did
was photobomb & call it
tough love   If *I'm still a breath*
to crackle & hiss through your hair
like a needle on vinyl
If warmer in groove

You Forgot What You Meant When You Read What You Said

I sidearm your ears into the lake

like stones   You have every right to implode

You dare me to pull the fire alarm   stitched to your back   Your body

reverberates, a garage band B side   Shaken loose,

a turtle emerges   with a left ear

in tow (maybe yours), a golden loop   ringed around

his thinning neck   & years from now, you'll only ever send blank letters home

to an empty house   The way everything rattles

like a loose doorknob in your palms   My metallic ring of a heartbeat

slaps the inside of my skull   hummingbird fast,

& yours   drowns in the feedback static

of a transmission lost too soon   Slow-stepping   Coming in   *Do you copy*

do you copy

Back to Your House

What is an appropriate reply to the sight of your waterlogged tongue: buds

budding   ripe pomegranate
seeds strung together into a rosary?

I lick clean   your uncontrollable
fears—forced to sing inside a birdcage,
large speakers toppling on you   On my phone, you're saved:

Even if that Tracheotomy came too late to save my pet turtle

The next night, I wear a sock as an ascot   the length of my neck

Looking for signs of life,

the Mars Rover snaps
a picture of us & Death   with this disquieting text:

Using your comb
on my inner thigh right now

The Way It Does in Bad Films

A radio bar of static pops & in your ID   imperfections   The bartender drags a discolored
tongue across the bar top, wipes clean my dead   skin, my wanting   to be left behind, to be the bread

crumbs & not the body so sure of the body it's owed   Some seats down, you fold yourself into a paper bird
missing one wing just as a mic boom dips into view   & Death's camera dolly rolls off its rails

Your body's ablaze, a life climaxing   in the perfect light   A folder stamped *repeat offender*:
every one of your bruising kisses, the stamp of a crumbling country

& I left my passportfeet by the front door
I look for you in my pocket   Shape talons out of your crumpled form

You Look Contorted on Yourself

When you tighten the bowtie around my aluminum   neck, the pressure pops off
bits of my lips I've spent   the last half hour puzzle-piecing back on

What's the point   My face is already stained
stale as a bar matchbook,
you argue, *& no one notices*   *the makeup*   How long

can I keep making up bone names & calling it a party
trick?   Are you better than that   you Frankenstein   spreading
ashes around the yard in a rainstorm   At some point, I'm hit by lightning,

my eggplant nose
purpling so fast &   you spray-paint
tear streaks down your cheeks   Last year, we signed yearbooks
like suicide pacts   The turning point: cherry picking

our organs from low hanging
tree limbs & off the concrete

THREE

Oh, This Could Be the Last Time So Here

is Death mass-texting news of its brain tumor for moral support

Attached, an Etch A Sketch MRI highlights
the lump, a heart   beating inside a skull   At home, leftovers

from a cleaned-out fridge spread across   nonexistent recollections
Death must now contemplate   *God,*

you make levitation look greasy   That afterbirth caked in the crook of your smirk
& me waiting   between the gym & life sciences building   my green booksack, my black
eye, my rusty veins   thinking we must spend our lives trying to be someone

else's exploding sun   In the meantime, I'm boring   the feathers off a nondescript species of quail
or possibly   just a rock with inordinate plumage   *Do you think I'd survive*

a war   a black hole   a field full of my own sordid love notes   I text Death back   *Your attention*
to detail though   Elsewhere, a child loses a few toy

soldiers in a red field: One, prone, wielding   a bayonet, while another will never stop
sweeping its metal detector over the dirt

I Still Don't Want to Stagger Home

How could anyone be good at playing dead?   All my friends are getting weird
with their bodies   yellow in the strangest

places, like a summer   I've wasted memorizing the names of the extra ghosts
clinging to your phantom limb   I'm trying to paint the picture, see:
I still had that hydraulic hunch when I walked, but my pulse   was more of a ringing
telephone wrapped in a blanket   When I saw you at the party, I swallowed my cell, waited for a

text from across the room   My stomach never once
buzzed   Then, waking
up the day after with my head hanging over like a cape   until it stopped, dropped,
& rolled off like a lopsided marble   My dumb body feeling around for it,
my head saying, *Find me   someone who doesn't deserve more*

or less of an afterlife & the whole   rest of the morning trying to erase
the blurred things my heart was doing at the time   tattooed down an arm
I'd never have guessed was   there, mine

Stand, You Can Sleep on the Plane

or at a bus stop   You rummage through your pockets when you realize you've misplaced
something staggering, ancient   Only a matter of time until you're all
Now where did my thumb go   Fallacy of the individual body,

I remind myself you are   the first human to survive
the peeling of an onion,   foam from the eyes

returning you to your cave, words clotting in your throat   & earlier, the old woman
at the grocery store grunting   as she unpouched her stomach to lay down
the day's vegetables at the checkout   & her skin poured to the ground,
battered   Behind her, another man's milk
soured, & over the intercom: *Did you hear   the doctor gave Death*

just one hundred & eighty more suns
The tumor old enough to talk back now   *Do you copy*

Come in, do you copy & around me, all this flotsam

The Conversation's Winding Away

All my friends chorus-line   *Don't make us wait*

in the tall   grass, wringing the sweat   from my shirt,

the shirt from my shirt   Deep down,

we both know

there aren't enough

belts in the world   to keep this car suspended

down the road   I give my wings to a half-buried baby

bird I stumble over

while, overhead, a plane explodes

My dear heart,   you tell me, *let's be brave*   but I'm ten years

late to a class reunion   & the PA system won't stop singing

the hits, noosing

your name   around

my neck

Come Home to This & with a Face

The embarrassment a train   must feel in front of everyone
when outscreeched by a man   at the tracks

handing out pinwheels made of bone for a living   Even the dumbest explosion
possesses the smarts   to say *I will only blow up this far*

The face of God   in the rearview mirror really clear
now, formed in the bruise on my face   A holy

hook & fishing line tangled,
streaming from my mouth out

the window   The tide   The hands dragging you back & off
the cliff edge where remembrance ends   Your world picking up speed around me   The radio speaks

a dead language   & when someone cuts me off, I yell   *No one ever thinks to ask*
how many light bulbs it takes to change a light bulb, do they, you asshole & out

the window goes my radioheart
with the wrong B-roll looped behind it

You're Drunk & the Kids

& the only person I've ever known   to sleep with a mouthful of crickets
tunnels his way out of my chest   a spoonful at a time until thick with placenta, holding a bouquet of roses

to my throat   I   SOS   If I spoon   the glimmer of this radio
long enough, will I be absorbed into its virgin static   Will I be a goose bump   on the arm of God

Tonight, a single cricket escapes from your mass to the ceiling & high dives into me
from a fan blade   I never thought I could choke on your echo,

your leathery chirps & applause   Fitting   but confounding how you say *I love you*
but really mean *effortlessness requires effort*   I'm yelling, asking

you to shine your thin light on me until I finish dyeing
my water bed sheets lifeboat orange   painting the ceiling a celestial letdown & all the while,

I wait for the wrenched-open faucet to fill up my head   I sleep best in a cold, wet room, a box of damaged
nerve endings under my bed   Your soul peels back my eyelids to leak

the water in search of its now bloated body, whispering something something
about perspective: *even a toy   soldier stays frozen in a real life   gunfight*

Sewn into Submission

In broad strokes, you paint a portrait of me squeezing   the light out of your sun   then smear
away my body with your palm   What's the worst thing I'll never be

able to unstick from my face   By now, the barista has bled   a hole
through my cup   with the tip of his marker   Growth would be me
not expecting you to show up   with your shadow unbuttoned

& I stare & those nightmares slowly running progress
are misery, are memory sewing   my eyes open

Life's sweeter that way,

but the rest of the afternoon I spend eating my words   turning papier-mâché
The chorus of papercuts when I press
my hands to my stomach have nothing to say about the black hole
where my head should be   & by my window, snowplows tear through town

in the middle of summer   Once thought impossible,
I run into everyone I could run into before sunset

There's Always This

Your hazmat suit shines   My shoelaces slump in knots
Smoke break ends early   as you hold my hand
as I hold your hand as I drop   the anchors
from my pocket   We window dive, skinny dip   the droplets
draining   out of your hair   There's always a reason to let a ghost
bleed out   always a horse opera hero hoping to stage
a comeback in a primetime slot decades after the show's off air

If you could keep the death wishes down,
I'd sew tweed patches over the moth-eaten holes
in my cheeks   dust off this old head
I haven't worn in forever   lower the radio to keep your sandal slap
in earshot   & admire the way you walk
into tattoo parlors naked   to signal
I'll take one of   everything you got!

FOUR

Leave Impossible Tasks

A sheet of instant film   My eyes locked on the sun

I should see a doctor   My ticker, the ball in an aerosol can   How much worse

could the rust around my ankles get   Stolen goods

from a garage sale: a toaster & someone else's

exsanguinated ghost   Frayed cords in tow, I resolder a camera to my hand

The Mars Rover zooms into the mirror, tight-

lensed, yelling *Action*, yelling *Action*

figure   So how'd I get so particular about bathrooms, you asked,

then *Leave*   *out the meaning this time*   I held back

your hair—   fished your ear out of the lake

nights before   cupped it close enough to hear   you slide into a red ocean

If You're Worried about the Weather

If a knife wound
tattoo is all it takes to pull
together   this look
If down the back of an ear,   fingertips beaded with sweat
If wrapped in cellophane   If I can't hear anything
outside of my own voice   my own voiceless—
If you're swimming through an argument
in laugh tracks   If a handful of your yellowing

teeth dropped in a vase,   nutrients for roses
If it's called *hide-&-go-*

nothing   when left in the cupboard
If you donate blood to a specter
through a straw until   you pass out
If the sky's more   penny than pound

Up Late but If You're Worried

All my friends pack together ash castles on the beach after
a bonfire   spit for mortar   & the ocean rolls back
home   stomach knotted   to pick through the day's
personals   There is such a sunlight   Stained

glass skin   Next to me   in my pew,
a fly genuflects & the echo   cathedral-wide
deafens   only to be drowned by the organ groaning

A kid with crossed legs holding his crotch   hands me a basket   my shame is a single dollar
All I want is the morning paper   My blood stuttering

in the sunlight   The sky so heady, thinking the world of itself   On my front porch,
one neighbor kid   triages the other neighbor kids
after a game of cops & robbers   I walk back inside

without the paper   without my arm,
my one good hand in my pocket   It comes out addled

Days in the Middle

An actor on TV   reportedly dying something fierce &   a last
wish for the doctor to pull out   a cell phone to film   the scene

Sometimes, I feel like a rock
God accidentally roved up to   a waste of binary
waves on their way home   Deep in His transistors,

would He regret thinking a universe of me   that I could resurrect anything

The wind   is off-key, & buried in a red throne
the Mars Rover phones home, toneless telegram   *I can see*
signs of water & life & I am really doing it   oh, creator what you said you couldn't

What about a mirror makes us feel present or not at all?

You Drop the First Ten Years Just as Fast as You Can

I'm the rain man of counting eyelashes

About that year in high school—these neon
sideburn scars will never
go away   & you're still eating that makeup wrong

Across the table   I am calling home
each time I open a phone book
& slam my finger down on a different
page number   I never knew Death

had class reunions, sweat   spots, got nervous   Did you
sleep best when you were someone's favorite

nuance   when you were the hurricane
nobody thought to name

If It's Crowded, All the Better

We live in a world   where the TV tells us
the passage of time is nothing more than expository

hair change—so why pretend   we're good at acting   On the subject,
a weakness: you lure me into the bathtub   by throwing in rice (of this, I am not
proud)   But we're all adults here, heavily   invested, nodding   fervently at
a bathroom stall made of mirrors   None other than a sex thing   donning civil war faces

Millions of hands
holding your purse   You keep
your apparition on a leash & that's mighty

considerate   but then line the tub
with barbed wire & pray   Water turns to wax & we lose track of my skin
at the bottom of the basin   This is growing old   *Are you*

almost done   with my favorite song
Afraid of black leather   *Want to get out of here*   & who wouldn't
recognize a loved one's scent   on a butcher's apron

Your Ridiculous Prop

Today, I'll have to make a real show of grabbing
the paper   Maybe two-handed, a sword   *Let's try desperately to keep the swollen*
word out of the conversation   *please*

Become your worst
origami nightmare—   fold my shirts
into cranes   & if you plan to keep that vision

around, then know I'm as alarmed as they come,
an aluminum boy   in a dream
shouting   *You were my morning*

shave, my torn page, my plastic bag stretched too holey,
etc   Did I tell you the neighbor
kids ate the last newspaper   alive   (hence, the theatrics)

You kiss me on the eyelids   & I'm really good at listening
as if I mean it

It's Better When We Pretend

Did you read the funnies today   Everywhere around us   the universe contracts
a cold   Sneezing out stars, planets, comets   *This is a real asthma attack*

of a bar you've picked   Restroom rehearsal   twelve cigarettes in my mouth, the words
underwater   Is the toilet spilling over   Is someone beating off
the hinges of this stall   Next door   in a theater,

the decomposed actor can't remember her lines

or parts   & at arm's length, her director signals the undisputed   symbol for stop, drop, &
roll over   A possum

on the side of the road   A million-dollar picture
deal in the pocket of a poorly fitting human   suit

We Set Controls for the Heart

Death in a pair of skinny jodhpurs sulks off screen   Tickles my ears with its riding crop   The skeletal
closeness of a memory   framed through bony fingers   when I become this

body of refugees   Between whose cushions
will you one day find my body   A copper piece, face
erased, a long-lost limb holding a red cup   bouquet & impossible

to love anymore   *Hello, this is my heart*
Remember when I controlled even the birds   fed them from the growth

on your shadow   A carpet stained with moldy   emotions where you shoulder me to the front,
soldier me to my knees, solder some scrap metal over my frame   How useless a Mars Rover
metaphor seems right now   So why don't you save me   for later   Let the birds

watch, wing   in wing   A love note
clicks on loud underfoot, a vest of cassette players taped to my chest with a laugh track of people
crying   & Death shouts *Action* shouts *Action* shouts *Action*

You Think Over & Over "Hey, I'm Finally Dead"

From atop this apartment   complex, people don't
look like ants   Easiest to pick you out—boom   in one hand, camera
in the other, & a gun in the holster

How to explain to people it's a big deal   my pet turtle won't respond
to a single anagram of its name   can't grasp
the soul's geometry   My spine, a rosary
ready   to snap & spill & other bones

popping loose now like taut suspenders   Five words:
will anyone see my wings   I'm the worst at charades
but not acting   It's why I'm up here   & I'll write the words on bathroom
stalls around the city until

you become gospel   *Who first said*
dying is that thing   which endlessly crumples us into ourselves until we roll back out
in the sunlight—all edges at first   then softer—

because they lied

The Moral Kicks In

After the first course, your corsage   flatlines into beautiful convulsions   It sprouts wings, thorns, claws

its way up your arm to swallow you goosebump   by goosebump   There is a moment when resurrection

devours the most devout heart   Deep blue   the ink pen veins blow up behind my eyes   Patron saint of stifling

anger   Patron saint of politely   melting into this tomato   soup a spoonful at a time

& we speak   in fortune cookie all night   The next dish, a ventilator   An IV   dripping into something

already dead   I order two specials   *Make the pain remind you of the one who signed your tiny*

gashes today   A struggling creek, your tongue

wriggles out from the baby's   breath to ask   *Were we ever anything*

more than   *echolocation*   Patron saint of the meteor that falls from the sky: forgiven, eventually, easily

Our Feet, You Spent the First Five

With whatever's left of these ash-caked   hands, I will love my monster   its marble organs   stumbling into the street
on cue, letting loose   a flood of epileptic eyes—glass of my glass, rolling down the driveway

If common courtesy is as simple as   pulling back someone's seat
even when   it's an electric chair then   *Look—I love you*
I look   for you in pictures before I look for myself   Our last meal

in the middle   of the street   We sign a fragile ceasefire down   your arm but not before you pour
the last   tub of toy soldiers onto the blistering   asphalt, veins in a frenzy, plastic screams
ripping a new road   through my mind   I dig my feet in & read   the morning paper to find out if they ever caught

us   Is it true we need another person in order to know we're real   Alight in a shelling of fireflies,
we eye each other's imperfections, & I ask you again (*I love you*)   *if you're going to end me*

Except in Parts

Inside my skull, your rendering is incomplete   Your shadow
clumsy   & all lung in that dress   When I try to remember you   too closely, the pixelation,   the crevices
where your squares meet like little   whispers lodged in skin

If it weren't for the half-finished puzzle   you started on my face, I'd guess
the world was ending   or beginning   If it weren't for that
smile   Tell me I'm your favorite

TV rerun   Nights before, your head pressed to my head
praying to hear footsteps   You drew an X across
the square of my chest, said *hold still,*   *I'm trying to dig*

my way out   of this CGI shell, a gaunt
pity of bone vectors
Nothing to enhance here   but why was I surprised
the deeper you burrowed, more of you   becoming more of me, splitting into finer
lines   *Hold on, I'm trying*   with nowhere to zoom in

That's How It Starts

Still, you   keep texting what is surely
the world's longest single-word soliloquy

I'll be home by the end of it—burnt to the filter, sweating
ash—but you   chronic combustible

will dart through the crowd waving those pinwheels   *Hello*
I'm still a breath   made of bone forever   You metronome, you   firework, the red

flushing down your neck like a wine-
stain   It isn't enough (watching

a spider's trapeze from corner to corner,
your memory rippling thinner & thinner)   to just forward the chain letter

about a child with cancer—obvious, but here
it is in a poem   My whole generation   combing

a hand through its hair   *Notice me*   *Notice me*
not

Weather, Then You Picked the Wrong Place to Stay

Bagging fall's last pile of leaves, the dew   soaking

my shoes, & the water   moccasin nestled at the heart of it all   Could memory be

so simple   Your ghost more afraid of me than I am of it   Here we are,

you wrapping a plastic bag around my head   my tongue trying

to poke a hole through the past   Should I mention I like what you've done with your hair

Taking this chance to impress you, scrawled   across my palm   *Don't look away at dinner*

when her jaws like a cartoon bear trap tear apart her lamb shank

If all memory is just the desire   to kill someone or something   *should I melt the butter*

or sharpen the butter knife instead   *Mirrors help to heal*

phantom limbs   & same as baby teeth   our earliest tattoos unlatch   so what of us

will not fall away in the minds of others   *We've already conceived of the atomic*

bomb so fuck the table settings

Fork goes on the inside or outside   *of the body*

FIVE

Where Are Your Friends Tonight

Peeling back the skin of the town   the mosaics throb like a mass   The Madabawi house
turned museum   The ground where my father lay left   little craters,
an imprint, a foreign system   a cancer too   In your living
room, all my friends peel shadows off the ground   like old carpet   Time—once

a frightened animal in the corner—now a rabid mouth   A bee traps itself under my shirt,
& another orbits a breathless   moon

Tell me the difference   between a velvet rope, an electric fence, a soldier warning *another step
closer* &   a frightened animal releasing a spurt of ink

The little bird pecking holes   in my father's little kid lungs   Now, he watches a doctor pin
his ghost   between a cold stethoscope & colder art saying   *You've swallowed
a sparrow* or *Tuberculosis*   Fighting its way out of your mouth, the unsuspecting

LSD strip expels itself & all my friends abandon body while I chip away at recollections
of you   I shake fists at little rocks, knowing the rocks never thought much of me anyway

Where Are Your Friends Tonight

All my friends drop off   Their droning
continues   Their crumbled heads,

pumpkins the morning after Halloween   *Oh, my beautiful smithereens lodged between*
your teeth   Is it what's left of them that carries me   I want to be a revered
peanut on the backs of ants, a molten   calf hoisted up a mountainside   Hear it implode

I'm afraid   *the science fair has gone awry*   Has God   fallen
asleep   at the projector   The following montage: ribbon-clad kids
going up in smoke   in the flameflashbang of an old-timey camera   in a thick
cloud of chalk clapped out by a hand from above   In the margins   a prescription

for sleeping pills   Me, under the stethoscope, everything sounding like the afterlife   The doctor
removes shards of you from my skin like splinters, sews my face back onto my face

& asks if my arm was always a camera   *Take eight of these at a time*, he says,
until visions cease

Where Are Your Friends Tonight

Even the birds can't find it in their bones
to sing for food today

Is it easier   from inside a cage   While the neighbor kids sell lemonade   to the leaves,
I ask for a portrait   Suddenly, I'm being framed
for the thumbtacks Death left in your chair   right before God shot me

a text to say   *It'll be ironic*
when all their oversized
hearts detonate against the insides of their ribcages   Birds
fatter & fatter & pop

On the downbeat in that hospital   bed, your mechanical breathing
reminds me of a little world's surface   cratering out of existence   Does the universe even care?

God answers: *Don't forget the twelve*

bucks you owe me this year   & I'm trying to put into words the euphoria of entering a space through an exit-
only door   What have I ever loved too much?

If I Could See All My Friends Tonight

Oh, dear

God, I'm wilting   don't feel

alive   (again)—   The number of times

I've thrown pennies   at the canary in my vacated

skull—still somehow chirping   its ragged

rhythm   shivering, nude—   to make it

go away

I can't look it   square in the eye but owe it

my eyes

Every few seconds, the whole world crowds around

the drag of your cigarette & then

darkness inhales our dim

silhouettes   but when you touch me—   the blowing out of light

bulbs in my chest   The burning bouquet you rooted there

If I Could See All My Friends Tonight

How you sit there & swear
gravity like God is just in   the air   The cold
flattens your eyes   A mind once removed   A green firetruck
blares by

I ask   *Was I for hours last night ironing out*
the creases of your windswept origami
wing   Yes, folding, refolding,   & brushing

the last ash   from your hair, dragging
littler selves to bed, walking backwards up the stairs   with you
swinging off the chandelier

I wonder if   a burning house, the wallpaper
melting, is the most beautiful place to be color-blind

If I Could See All My Friends Tonight

Ordering your dinner   you say
the most disposable things at the little Italian cafe

Cigarette burn this, *motion sickness* that

I begin with a joke   *What's the difference between God*
& the Mars Rover   Rumor has it

Death deals with dandruff same as us & sheds
skin in the shower, too
Your mouth

a cacophony of movie set sounds   I make
a mental note: *there was a sky*   *but no explanation*
I helped you into the cab

You, so filmy   Your hair too grainy   You, so black-&-white &
deep, it hurt

If I Could See All My Friends Tonight

From my window, your many   faces refract

light into jittery colors, your drunken seams   unthread in the wind

Impossible
to be sure   if anything will be left   to photograph in this world

I've taken up reading
palms by the crateful   Place palm over palm
& compress   my lifeless sun, feel wooden beams
splinter

The sun coughs up blood & breath
across my smile   Leave
the dark of the night to me   I'll make sure it gets home safe

SIX

You Always Knew You were Tired

If I have to   relearn   my body I will
with a mother's amazement   clapping together her baby's feet

If with a mother's amazement clapping together her baby's feet
I relearn my body—

NOTES

All of the titles from this manuscript are taken, in some fashion, from the lyrics of "All My Friends" by LCD Soundsystem.

In "I Still Don't Want to Stagger Home" & "It's the Memory of Our Betters," the final lines are slight variations of a line from the poem "Away" by Raymond Carver.

The words "Fallacy of the individual body" in "I Still Don't Want to Stagger Home" are a slight variation of the phrase "Fallacy of the local body" from Richard Siken's poem "The Way the Light Reflects."

The phrase *"using your comb on my inner thigh right now"* from the poem "Back to Your House" was taken from a note that Leo Costigan left for me on the dinner table of our apartment in graduate school.